Mabel In The Woods and Other Plays

Nine Monologue Plays by Don Nigro

A SAMUEL FRENCH ACTING EDITION

SAMUEL FRENCH
FOUNDED 1830

SAMUELFRENCH.COM
SAMUELFRENCH-LONDON.CO.UK

FOR PRODUCTION ENQUIRIES

UNITED STATES AND CANADA
Info@SamuelFrench.com
1-866-598-8449

UNITED KINGDOM AND EUROPE
Plays@SamuelFrench-London.co.uk
020-7255-4302

Each title is subject to availability from Samuel French, depending
upon country of performance. Please be aware that *MABEL IN THE
WOODS AND OTHER PLAYS* may not be licensed by Samuel French in
your territory. Professional and amateur producers should contact the
nearest Samuel French office or licensing partner to verify availability.

MUSIC USE NOTE

CONTENTS

Mabel In The Woods

For Anna Contessa

CHARACTER & SETTING

There is one character, **BEN**, a tall man in his late fifties, who speaks to us from his study, in a house by the woods.

(BEN, a tall man in his late fifties, speaking to us from his study.)

BEN.

Mabel had some vivid but confused memories of her kittenhood: of feeling safe and warm cuddled up with her mother and two sisters, of crawling about under a snowball bush behind a red house where an old woman lived and put out food for them. And there was one memory she especially cherished: of being in the house, curled up on a rug at the feet of the old woman while bright colored pictures and voices came from a big box against the wall, of a hand running across her back and scratching behind her ears, and of someone dragging a string back and forth across the rug while she chased it. She remembered being blissfully happy there.

But then one night a big white truck with a flashing red light pulled up by the house, making a terribly loud noise, while Mabel huddled with her mother and sisters under the snowball bush. Then there was another car with a flashing light, and men rushing in and out of the house, and then two men emerged, carrying the old woman away, lying very still and white.

The next morning, for the first time in her life, there was no food in the bowls by the back door. There was no food that afternoon, or that evening. Mabel's mother went hunting, and brought a mouse, but it was hardly enough for all of them. Her mother didn't eat, just looked on with worried eyes. There was no food the next day, or the next, and at night the house was dark and silent. They began to get very hungry.

Then one night something terrible happened, that Mabel never liked to think about afterwards. Made bolder by the old woman's absence, a coyote came in

7

the night. It was all confusion and panic then. The four cats scattered in all directions. Mabel was overwhelmed with terror. She didn't know where she was running. At one point she dashed across a creek on a fallen log and some stones. Then she found herself in deep woods. She ran and ran until, on a steep wooded hillside, she stumbled into an old tree with a big hole in it, and hid herself there, her heart pounding. She huddled there trembling for a long time, and eventually fell asleep.

In the morning she looked out from the tree and saw the woods all around her. It had rained heavily overnight, and the woods smelled so rich and strange. She had no idea where she was. She meowed for her mother, her sisters, but nobody answered. She was completely alone.

She was very hungry, but she managed to find a few insects to eat. The hole in the tree offered some protection from the weather, and as she grew brave enough to venture farther from the hollow tree, she began to get a sense of the geography of the thickly wooded hillside. It was easy to get lost at first, but she found some big rocks that seemed to have been placed in a line from west to east across the middle of the hillside long ago, for some purpose Mabel could not imagine. She thought of them as the Marker Rocks and by following them she found her way to the west part of the hillside, where the paths became hopelessly tangled in wild grape vines that created a thick barrier for larger animals. And below the Marker Rocks, to the southeast, was a deep ravine that led down towards the driveway of a long, tan house. The ridge of the hill was her northern boundary, the grape vines on the west, the ravine on the east, and the back yard of the house at the foot of the hill to the south: this was her territory, and she never ventured out of it. She found the woods beautiful, but very dangerous. She liked to listen to the birds sing, and watch the deer nibbling at tender young leaves. But she was always afraid. A small creature like herself couldn't let her guard down for a moment in the woods.

She didn't know how long she'd lived on the wooded hillside when the other cat appeared. He was a big old filthy brownish creature with many battle scars. She hissed at him at first, and avoided him, but also found herself mysteriously drawn to him, and in the course of time, long after the tomcat was gone, she felt something stirring inside her, and one rainy afternoon she gave birth to four kittens in the old tree. There were three boys: Yellow Cat, an energetic light orange tabby; Albert, a thoughtful mackerel tabby who resembled his father; and Louie, a shy, gray striped tabby. And there was a little daughter, Cookie, who, like Mabel, was a pure tortie—mostly dark brown and black with fragments of harlequin pattern and a touch of cream color here and there. Mabel found herself hopelessly in love with her kittens, and something inside her seemed to know how to take care of them, the way her mother had taken care of her. It was so nice to have company again, someone to love and watch out for. But she was terrified every moment that they would not survive in the woods, and she began to understand that when you love something, you can never rest easy again.

Sometimes, when she was out hunting, she'd go up to a special place thick with ferns towards the northeast corner of her territory, where the ridge of the hill flattened out a bit, to watch the trees move when there was no wind, and listen to an eerie buzzing sound when there were no bees. She would go there to try and remember what it was like before she came to the woods, in the other place, where she'd lived with her mother and sisters under the snowball bush. She felt her best memories fading, and then she would think of the truck and the car with the red flashing lights, and the terrible night when the coyote came, and she decided remembering was too sad.

One day, when her kittens were about three weeks old, she heard a loud, distressed mewling in the woods. Puzzled, she saw that her own children were all cuddled up together sleeping in the hollow tree, and went to investigate. Behind a sumac tree near the top of an old logging path she found two black kittens, Fuzzy and Panther. They looked exactly the same, except that Fuzzy had long, beautiful hair, while Panther's coat was shorter, sleek and shiny. Where they had come from, or what had happened to their mother, Mabel never knew, but when they saw her, they ran to her, mewling and squalling, desperate to nurse. Her first instinct was to hiss at them. She was having enough trouble nursing her own four kittens. She was still little more than a kitten herself. The last thing she needed was two more boys, bigger than hers, stealing her precious milk.

Fuzzy and Panther were shocked when she growled and batted them away, but it didn't stop them for long. Soon they were back, nuzzling under her, looking for breakfast. And Mabel found, against her better judgement, that she could not bring herself to turn her back on them. Something inside her melted when she felt their desperate little noses pressing into her fur, and in the end, she let them follow her back down the logging path to the hollow tree to nurse along with her own four.

But the extra mouths to feed were only making worse what was already becoming an increasingly desperate situation. Mabel went out hunting constantly, trying to nourish herself enough to feed the six kittens. She felt herself growing thin and raggedy. Her coat was patchy. She was weak. But she did the best she could. And after a time, the kittens began to chase and eat beetles and crickets, but still there never seemed to be enough food for everybody.

And the kittens were always getting into trouble. She worried about them constantly, and she was always having to rescue them from one near disaster or another. Yellow Cat had an especially adventurous disposition, and Cookie would tag after him wherever he went. Albert was prone to fits of melancholy and sometimes would sit brooding at night, looking at the moon. Louie was afraid of everything, even his own tail on occasion, and he idolized the somewhat bigger and very furry Fuzzy, who was nearly as terrified of things as Louie, but would sometimes forget to be afraid when he was playing. Panther was the smartest of the kittens, and the most curious. It was Panther who was to bring them into contact with the tall man. This is how it happened:

At the foot of the hill, the woods turned into a yard with evergreens, a big sassafras tree covered with honeysuckle, and the long, tan house, surrounded by more evergreens and fire bushes. In the west part of the yard, near the house, was a dead tree that, when viewed from a certain angle, looked to Mabel like an angry demon. She saw this as a sign that whoever lived in the house must be evil. She discouraged her children from ever going into the open yard, where she knew they would be easier for hawks and coyotes to spot. But there was a little patch of weeds just north of the sassafras tree, at the foot of the ravine, where apple cores, corn cobs, and other such things sometimes appeared. The raccoons, the possums and groundhogs would go there to scavenge, and Panther could not resist investigating, to see what new things had mysteriously appeared on the little pile. One day what he found was some chicken wings. He couldn't believe his good luck, chewing off the few strands of meat left on them, and soon Fuzzy was eating with him, and then Yellow Cat and Cookie. Mabel was certain it must be some sort of trap, but the kittens were getting big enough to hunt on their own, and there was no way she could stop them. Eventually Albert and Louie also began going down to the magical spot, where they would all hide in the bushes, waiting for chicken wings to appear.

One day they were startled to discover a tall person striding towards them. They all froze in the bushes, watching in horror, ready to bolt. The tall man threw something onto the pile and went back towards the house. When they were sure he was gone, Panther and Yellow Cat came out to look. It was pork chops. The man had thrown the remains of pork chops on the pile. The kittens were in heaven. Nothing in the world had ever tasted so good to them. From then on, the most exciting part of the day was waiting for the tall man to come out of the house with a new treat for them. Mabel did her best to talk them out of it, but the kittens wouldn't listen to her. And one day, when they saw the tall man coming, Fuzzy and Panther got so excited they forgot to hide. They sat on a log while he threw chicken bones on the pile. The man turned and looked them. They froze, watching him. Then Fuzzy bolted and disappeared into the bushes. But Panther remained sitting on the log, looking back at the tall man.

Where did you come from? said the tall man. He did not sound very friendly, and they had never seen him smile. But Panther just stared at him, fascinated by his first close look at a human being. From the bushes, Mabel and Fuzzy were watching, terrified that the tall man would swoop down on Panther and devour him. But the tall man just turned and walked back towards the house.

In the days that followed, Yellow Cat and Cookie would join Fuzzy and Panther on the log, waiting for the tall man to appear. Mabel stayed hidden in the bushes with Albert and Louie. She tried to convince them not to trust the tall man. Her life thus far had taught her that if you want to survive, don't trust anybody. But the kittens loved the chicken wings and steak bones and wouldn't listen. After a while, Albert and Louie would also wait on the log for the tall man, all six kittens lined up in a row. Only Mabel would stay hidden. She thought if the tall man did try to hurt them, her best strategy would be to leap out of the bushes onto his back and bite his neck. In the woods, if it's smaller than you, it's prey. If it's bigger than you, it's a predator. She was certain the man was just trying to lull the kittens into a false sense of security so he could do something terrible to them.

This suspicion was confirmed when one day the man put a couple of old dishes under the sassafras tree with the honeysuckle growing up it and filled them with cat food. Mabel told her children not to eat it, that it was probably poisoned, but it smelled good, and soon they were gobbling down the stuff. Eventually, she came over and tried a bite. It wasn't bad. But still, she decided, it must be part of the tall man's plan to fatten them up before he devoured them.

Sometimes, when it rained, the food in the dishes would get all soggy and be ruined, so the tall man began putting the bowls by the back door of the house, under the overhanging part of the roof, near the old red brick patio, and the kittens got used to coming down by the back door to wait for food. Mabel stayed behind the chestnut tree, watching over them.

Now and then, when the tall man would go out to work in the yard, he'd leave the back door open, and Yellow Cat and Panther would sneak into the garage to have a look around. Mabel warned them it was a trap, but they ignored her. She peered in, and saw two old automobiles, a white one and a brown one. She had never seen either of these actually run. The tall man usually drove a newer red car that was parked in the driveway, or the old black truck beside it. She found the smells from the garage disturbing. She was never at ease until her kittens had run out of there and back up into the woods.

Sometimes Panther would sit nearby and watch the man dig in the yard, or replace bricks in the patio. The man would talk to Panther as he worked, explaining what he was doing. Panther didn't know why, but he liked watching the man work, and he liked having the man talk to him. He liked keeping the man company.

One early autumn afternoon, Mabel and all six kittens were lying around under the chestnut tree in the sun. Some were playing, and some were dozing. Then Mabel sensed that something was watching them. She looked up and saw the tall man staring at them through the back window of the house, with a serious look on his face. It was clear to her that he was thinking about them. What he was thinking, she couldn't be sure.

The next day the tall man went out to work in the yard and left the back door to the garage open behind him, and one by one, Yellow Cat, Panther, Cookie and Louie, who was feeling unusually brave, snuck into the garage to explore. Then, to her horror, Mabel saw the man walk back in the door and close it behind him. Four of her children were trapped in the tall man's garage.

She waited and waited for the tall man to come out again. She wanted to sneak in the garage and rescue her children. But when the tall man did come out, it was only to bring with him an odd cage-like device, which he put some food in. Then he went back inside. When he was gone, she went over to examine the little metal cage-like thing. It was like a long box, with one end open, and the tall man had put the food at the far end, away from the opening. Fuzzy and Albert came over to sniff at it with her. Albert thought about going inside the cage to get the food, but then got scared, and went back up into the woods. But Fuzzy was very hungry. Mabel tried to persuade him not to go in, but he really wanted the food, so he walked into the cage-like box. Nothing happened. He took another step, and rested his front paws on the little sloped piece of metal in front of the food. There was a loud clang that scared both of them. Mabel ran behind the fire bush. Fuzzy tried to follow her, but now, suddenly, there was no way to get out. Fuzzy began to panic. He clawed back and forth, trying desperately to force his way out of the cage. Mabel was running back to help him when the side door of the garage opened and the tall man came out. He picked up the cage, with Fuzzy in it, took it into the garage, and closed the door behind him. Mabel stood there, looking at the closed door. The tall man had stolen five of her six children.

She went around the corner to the front of the garage. and put her nose down by a space under the big white door. A paw shot out in her direction. It was Yellow Cat. Then another, mottled like hers. It was Cookie. So they were still alive, at least. She stayed there at the big doors until she'd made some sort of contact with all five. They were afraid, but unharmed.

Then she heard the side door open again, and the metal clang of the cage being set down on the bricks. She ran and hid under the old truck until she heard the tall man go back into the garage. She went back to the big door, where Cookie was sticking her paw out. Maybe if she could just somehow scratch at the door until she'd made a hole in it. She was occupied with this when she heard the metal clang again. And then she realized: Albert. She looked around the corner just in time to see the tall man carrying the cage, with the frantic Albert, into the garage, and close the door behind him.

Mabel was in despair. This monster had stolen all her children from her, leaving her alone again. Then she heard the door open, and the sound of the cage being put on the bricks, and of the man going back into the garage. She looked around the corner. There was the cage, with a fresh can of tuna placed carefully in the same place. She went over and examined the cage carefully. She thought and thought about it. All she wanted was to be with her children. Working up her courage, she stepped into the cage, and deliberately put her front feet on the slanted metal panel. Down came the end of the cage. She was trapped.

She had known what she was doing, but now that she was trapped, her instincts took over, and she panicked. She tried desperately to claw her way out. She was actually able to move the cage from side to side by hurling herself back and forth, and once it almost tipped. Then the door opened, the tall man came out, picked up the cage, and brought her into the garage. Mabel thought: I'm going to die with my children.

The tall man closed the door behind them, and put the cage down. He was talking to her quietly, but she was in no mood to listen. She just wanted out. She hissed and growled at him when he put his hand down towards the cage. Carefully he pulled up a latch and opened the cage door. Then he stepped back. Mabel looked at the tall man, then at the sudden open space, then back at the tall man again. She knew it must be a trick. But she wanted to see her children. All that mattered was that she should be with her children. She took a deep breath and then bolted out of the cage, running under the old white car. She was able to crawl up under the back bumper and hide herself, her heart pounding. She realized then that Fuzzy was huddled there beside her. She licked his face. He licked her back. He was trembling. She'd never seen him so upset. She kept licking him until he calmed down.

When the tall man had gone into the house, Mabel cautiously let herself down from inside the back bumper of the old car and began to look around, and one by one, all of them appeared. Cookie and Panther and Yellow Cat and Louie and Albert. Fuzzy was reluctant to come out at all. But everybody seemed all right, and Mabel discovered that there was food and water under a bench by the door that led into the house. If the door opened and the tall man came out, they could just scatter under the two old cars and hide up inside them until he went away.

The next few days were quiet. The tall man kept them supplied with food and water, and there were boxes filled with clay along the north wall where they could relieve themselves. If you jumped up onto the cars, you could look out the window at the field by the house, and up at the woods. You could also see the woods out the window of the back door. And there were two big windows that faced south. So Mabel could still keep track of what was going on in this part of her territory. The tall man had put out a chair with a soft rug on it, and Mabel jumped up, found that it was very comfortable, and went to sleep there. Her now half grown kittens took turns cuddling with her, and there was also a picnic table with some rugs on it, and a couple of plastic carrier things with towels in them, so there were many cozy places to curl up. At night, everybody came out and explored, even Fuzzy. But during the day they would all run and hide when the door opened. Fuzzy hid in the big white car at dawn and would not show himself until late at night, when it was clear that nobody was stirring in the house.

After a while, when the tall man appeared, if he didn't move directly towards her, Mabel would stay in her chair, looking at him with great suspicion, waiting for him to make a move. But he would just say hello to her, and to the other cats, and go out the side door, which he always kept closed. She could only presume that the tall man was putting out all this food so he could fatten them up and eat them. She could think of no other reason for his odd behavior. In the woods, either you ate something, or it ate you.

But to her increasing unease, the kittens were not so relentlessly suspicious. Being kittens, they wanted to play when they weren't eating or sleeping, and would chase each other all over the garage, leaping from one old car to the other, across the picnic table or up on the work bench. She liked to watch them play, and was pleased that they were happy, but she knew the tall man was giving them a false sense of security. This was another thing she had learned in the woods: an animal which is not alert, cautious and suspicious at all times is sooner or later a dead animal.

And then the tall man began doing a very curious thing. There was a set of concrete steps that led from the back door down under the work bench to the basement of the house. Now and then, the tall man would come up those concrete stairs and drop a long piece of clothesline over the edge of the little concrete wall the work bench rested on. He would stay hidden on the steps behind the wall, and move the clothes line back and forth. The kittens were hypnotized by this, and soon began chasing the bit of clothes line. Yellow Cat, Panther and Cookie loved this game, and played it with increasing enthusiasm. Mabel remained on her chair, watching in disapproval, convinced that the tall man was going to strangle them with the clothes line. Albert and Louie watched the play with great interest, but were too scared to join in. And Fuzzy remained hidden in the white car.

This game with the clothes line happened every day, and the kittens all looked forward to it. Gradually, the tall man allowed them to see his hand over top of the wall, and then his head, and after a few days he was able to lean over the wall while he moved the clothes line back and forth on the concrete. The kittens were having a wonderful time. Albert and Louie were starting to shyly join in. But Mabel just looked on, more and more worried.

Then one day an extraordinary thing happened. The tall man was whipping the clothes line back and forth on the concrete, and the kittens were galloping wildly after it, when suddenly a large black paw reached out from under the white car and grabbed the clothes line. It was Fuzzy. He'd been listening to all this playing going on, and Fuzzy was a cat who loved to play. After a while he just couldn't stand it any more. He had to chase the clothes line. At first he was cautious, staying under the car while the others ran back and forth. But the tall man would whip the clothes line under the car now and then, and Fuzzy would jump on it. After a few days, he was coming out to play with the others. His days of cowering inside the white car were over.

And the surprising thing was, once Fuzzy had come out from inside the white car, he seemed to lose his fear faster than the others. Sometimes, when the cats raced by, the tall man had been gently letting the palm of his hand rest briefly on their backs. At first this alarmed them, but they were having so much fun, they didn't pay much attention to it. But Mabel noticed that Fuzzy would actually linger under the hand for longer than he needed to, pretending he was absorbed with the clothes line. He actually seemed to like the feel of the tall man's hand moving across his back. Mabel had always been worried about Fuzzy. Of all her children, he was the only one with long hair, and he had always made odd noises. He seemed to have his own strange vocabulary of yowly comments when he was playing with Cookie or Panther. And since he was the biggest of the kittens, Mabel thought Fuzzy would probably be the first one the tall man ate.

Then something even more alarming happened. The kitchen door had a screen door outside it, and sometimes the tall man would leave the inner door open so the kittens could come up on the concrete step and look through the screen. They could see some wooden cabinets, a table and some chairs. They had no idea what was beyond that. But they were very, very curious. Then one day, the tall man propped open the screen door and disappeared into the house.

One by one Mabel's kittens came up onto the concrete step. It seemed so strange that where there had been two doors, now there was nothing, and yet the kittens instinctively felt that there was still a barrier there. Cookie put her tiny little tortie foot in, then backed up. Yellow Cat walked away, then came back, unsure what to do. Finally, to Mabel's horror, Panther impulsively ran through the doorway and into the kitchen, then stopped, looking around, sniffing. The house smelled like the tall man, and something that had just been cooked, and wood and other things he couldn't identify. Mabel watched helplessly as Panther disappeared into the house.

He moved through a little bathroom area and found himself in a room with a large bed. It smelled even more like the tall man. Panther jumped up on the bed and lay down. It felt wonderful. He decided at that moment that the house was a good thing. Meanwhile, Yellow Cat had come into the kitchen, followed by Cookie. After a bit, Fuzzy came in, then went back out, then came in again. This was the beginning of a series of exciting exploratory trips into the house. Eventually, all of the cats, even the very timid Louie, were exploring the house except Mabel, who would sit just outside the kitchen door and watch, worrying, until her children returned from these adventures.

The tall man was always watching, from a little distance. He never interfered, but sometimes he would move down the hallway to have a look at what the cats were up to. Sometimes he would open the door at the foot of the concrete steps and let the cats explore the basement. Cookie was especially fond of the house, and sometimes would become so absorbed in her discoveries that she'd lose track of where the other cats were.

One night all of the cats had gone back out except Cookie, who was still in the far southwest corner of the basement, following a beetle. When she looked up and realized that none of the other cats were around, she forgot where she was, and where the door was, and how to get there, and she began to wail. She wailed and wailed. The tall man was standing by the wooden inner steps that led upstairs, looking at her.

Well, go on out, if you want to go out, said the tall man.

Cookie just wailed, and stayed where she was, in the dark corner with the now forgotten beetle. Mabel and Yellow Cat were at the bottom of the concrete steps, concerned about Cookie. Finally Yellow Cat came back in the door, made his way cautiously over to the rug in front of the old juke box, and stopped, seeing the tall man standing by the wooden steps, between him and the wailing Cookie.

Go and get your sister, said the tall man.

Yellow Cat hesitated.

Go on, said the tall man, gesturing to Yellow Cat as he spoke. Go get your sister. If you'll go get her, I'll stay right here.

Cookie wailed again. Yellow Cat looked towards the dark corner of the basement where Cookie's wailing came from, then at the tall man. Then he decided. He made his way carefully past the tall man, under the big oak table, and into the dark corner. From her place just outside the basement door, Mabel could hear the happy burbling of Cookie and Yellow Cat as they greeted each other. Then Yellow Cat trotted out under the oak table and past the juke box, followed by closely by Cookie. When Cookie had run past him, out the door to be greeted by Mabel, Yellow Cat turned and looked back at the tall man for a moment.

Good boy, said the tall man.

Yellow Cat looked at him for a moment longer, then turned and went out the door and back up the concrete steps into the garage with Cookie trailing after him. But Mabel stayed at the foot of the steps, looking at the tall man. He was a mystery she could not seem to solve.

She continued to be certain that it was all some sort of trick, and yet she liked not having to worry about food and predators all the time. She liked having all her children right there where she could see they were safe. She liked curling up on the chair, and looking out the window in the mornings. And sometimes she even liked watching her children play with the tall man.

And lately she'd been feeling odd stirrings. She began to dream about the woods, and about the old tomcat who had fathered her kittens. One day she woke up from such a dream and saw Panther staring at her. Something in the way he was looking at her reminded her of the old tomcat. Why was he looking at her like that? Probably he didn't know, either. She looked up and saw the tall man watching her and Panther.

The next day, when Mabel was lying in her chair, half asleep, she looked up to see that the tall man had quietly placed one of the cat carriers near by, and was reaching down towards her. This was it, she thought. He's finally attacking. She squirmed and fought, then got her mouth around one of the tall man's fingers and bit into it as hard as she could. The tall man yelled and immediately let her go. She ran and hid up under the white car.

Shortly after this, the kidnappings began. The tall man put some food in one of the cat carriers, and when Panther went in to get it, quickly closed the door. Mabel jumped up on the brown car and saw the tall man put the carrier, with Panther in it, in the back of his red car and drive away.

It's begun now, thought Mabel, grieving. He's going to start murdering us, one by one. She and the kittens passed a horrible day. Mabel was convinced she'd never see Panther again. But that evening, the tall man returned with the carrier, and something lay inside. It was Panther, but he seemed all drained of energy, and he smelled different. Something dreadful had happened to him. But the tall man did not release

Panther back into the garage. Instead, he took him into the house.

The next day, when the tall man opened the basement door, most of the cats were afraid to come in. But Cookie wanted to see Panther. She found him not far away, cowering under the old wooden bar, trembling, shaken, and miserable. Cookie began to lick him. Then she curled up beside him, and Panther cuddled with her. The tall man looked at them for a bit, then closed the door. It took Cookie a moment to realize that she was now trapped in the house. At first she panicked. She ran up the wooden steps to the kitchen door, but it was closed. Then she hid behind the refrigerator. But the tall man seemed to be paying no attention to her. He put out food and water, and left her alone. After a bit, she went back downstairs and curled up with Panther again. Panther seemed better. They snuggled all night.

The next day the tall man put food in the carrier again, and this time he was able to close the door on Yellow Cat, took him out to the red car, and drove off with him. And that evening, he returned, with Yellow Cat in the box, and took him into the house. Yellow Cat ran and hid under the bar, where Cookie found him. She licked his nose and cuddled up with him.

By now Mabel had convinced the other cats never to go into the cat carrier again, no matter how much food was there. The tall man kept trying to lure them in, but nobody would go. They didn't trust him any more. Then the metal trap appeared again. The man put food in it, and without thinking, Louie went right in to eat. The trap sprung, the end of the cage closed, and the tall man took Louie away in the cage. And that evening, the man returned with Louie, and took him into the house, where Cookie was waiting to greet him, and lick his face.

Now there were just Mabel, Fuzzy and Albert left in the garage. The next time the man put the trap out, Albert and Fuzzy were greatly tempted to go in. The man was now only putting food in the trap, and they were hungry. Mabel stationed herself in front of the trap and refused to let them pass. But they kept trying to push past her to get to the food. Just then, the tall man came out the kitchen door. Fuzzy and Albert ran out of the cage, but Mabel had instinctively backed up, and stepped on the sloping piece of metal. The end of the cage came down, and Mabel was trapped again. She fought like a maniac to get out. When the tall man picked up the cage by its handle, she tried to bite his hand again, but couldn't get to it. She tried to reach up and claw it. She was consumed with anger and terror.

All the while, the tall man was talking to her, quietly. He put the cage in the back of the red car, then went around front and got in. He started the car, talked to her while it was warming up, then began to back up. Mabel realized it was impossible to escape. She was filled with despair.

It was a short drive to another place that smelled of chemicals and dogs and fear, and Mabel hated it, but she was so exhausted, and so unhappy, that she no longer struggled. The tall man spoke to her softly, said goodbye, and they took her into a room full of cages filled with other cats and dogs. After what seemed like a very long time, someone picked up the cage, put it on a table, and opened it, wearing thick gloves. She felt herself being pulled out of the cage and onto a table, where she was held down and something was poked into her. After a bit, everything began to go away, and she slept. This is what dying is, she thought.

She dreamed that she was back in the woods. There was a deer, a raccoon, a crow, all of them friends, and her mother and sisters were there. Her mother was trying to tell her something, but Mabel couldn't make out what it was.

When she woke up, she was back in the room with all the cages, and her stomach hurt, and somebody had shaved off some of her hair. She just wanted to sleep. She closed her eyes, and when she opened them again, the tall man was carrying her out to the car. She didn't know how much time had passed. The man pulled into the familiar driveway, and took Mabel into the garage. She caught a glimpse of Albert and Fuzzy, looking at her, and then the man took her into the house.

It was the first time she'd been in the house. It reminded her of something she couldn't quite remember. He took her down the wooden steps and into the basement. There he let her see a row of litter boxes and some food, and then opened the door of the cage and walked away. Cautiously, Mabel crept out of the cage, then ran for her life, and hid under a cot. Soon she was greeted by Cookie, who was overjoyed to see her, kissing her and licking her and rubbing up against her. The tall man had gone away. Mabel looked out from under the cot and saw Panther, Yellow Cat and Louie. They all seemed fine. She thought perhaps she was still dreaming.

A couple of days later, the tall man brought Fuzzy and Albert into the house. They had both gone into the trap to get something to eat, and made the journey to the other place together. Albert was convinced he was going to die, but Fuzzy looked at the tall man's eyes, asking, silently, if it was going to be all right.

It's going to be all right, said the tall man. And Fuzzy, somehow, believed him. Albert trembled up against him, hiding his face in Fuzzy's thick, soft, black fur. But Fuzzy was strangely calm.

So now they were all seven back together, in the house. Albert was afraid for a while after his return, but Fuzzy was happy. Cookie took them on a tour, showing them all the best places to hide and to curl up. There were three bedrooms, a big room with many books, a kitchen, an entryway and two bathrooms. There was something interesting about every room. Cookie had discovered that if she jumped up on the table by the large back window in the big room, she had a great view of the back yard and the woods. It was her favorite place. And soon, one by one, the others began spending more time upstairs. Panther found the big bed, and lay on it. Fuzzy found a nice soft chair in the big room he liked especially. Yellow Cat liked the sofa, and Louie and Albert found cozy places under the beds in the spare bedrooms. And finally, after much hesitation, one afternoon when the tall man had gone out, Mabel came up the steps and began to explore the rest of the house.

There was food upstairs, in the kitchen, as well as downstairs. The house smelled good, and there was a sofa and a couple of soft chairs to curl up on. Fuzzy looked happy in his easy chair. Panther on his bed. And Cookie showed her how if she jumped up on the table she could see the woods. When the tall man returned, Mabel ran and hid from him, but the tall man just said hello and went about his business. He spent a lot of time in the basement, pressing his fingers down on a white thing and looking at a screen, or up in the living room, at the table by the back window, making marks in a notebook. Sometimes he would play with them, with a long piece of clothes line, and the kittens would run all over the kitchen chasing it. Mabel would have nothing to do with this. But more and more she was almost remembering something.

She would sit at the back window of the living room, looking out at the woods for hours, trying to understand what had happened to her, but she couldn't make any sense of it. Being in the house was actually much more comfortable than the garage had been, but she could not shake her suspicions of the tall man.

Then one day something extraordinary happened. Fuzzy had been spending a lot of time with the tall man, playing, following him about the house. Something in him seemed to crave the tall man's company. Whenever the tall man put out food, the others waited until he went away, but Fuzzy would be right there ready to eat. He would even lick gravy off the tall man's finger, the same one that Mabel had bitten. Then one day, when the tall man poured food into the bowl, Fuzzy brushed his arm, rubbing against it, and the tall man reached down and began to pet him. Mabel was horrified. None of them had ever deliberately allowed the tall man to touch them. The tall man ran his hand along Fuzzy's back, talking to him quietly. Then he began scratching under Fuzzy's chin. Fuzzy lay down on the rug and allowed the tall man to rub his tummy. He was purring and purring. Mabel couldn't understand it. It disturbed her because it reminded her of the old woman, but then immediately she saw the flashing lights, the men, the coyote.

The other kittens were fascinated by Fuzzy's acceptance of the tall man's caresses. They just didn't know what to make of it. Something in them wanted to try it, but their fear told them not to. So for a long time, Fuzzy was the only cat who let the tall man touch him. But Mabel watched them every day. And sometimes, looking out the back window at the woods, she would glance over at the tall man sitting at the wooden table with all the books, staring out at the woods himself, and one day it struck her, for the first time, that the tall man was lonely.

It had never occurred to her that he could possibly feel anything like what she felt. And yet the look on his face, as he sat there staring out at the woods, made her think he might actually have his own sorrows. She couldn't imagine what they might be. But from that time on, they would often sit together, the man at the table covered in books, and Mabel on the window sill, both looking out at the woods. Mabel began to feel a strange communion with the tall man. She watched him play with her children. He was kind to them, and very patient, and careful not to hurt them. He talked to them, and fed them, and played with them, and when Fuzzy came to him, he petted him as long as Fuzzy wanted.

In the evenings the tall man would sit in the chair in front of the big screen and watch colors moving back and forth in the box. It was all so much like what she remembered. Sometimes she would lie on the rug at his feet while he watched. Often he would speak gently to her. One night he said, You did a really good job, Mabel. You were very brave, and very strong, and you took good care of your children, and now everybody's safe and happy. You can relax now. You don't have to worry any more. It's all right.

And he reached down a hand, the same hand that she'd bitten before. Mabel shied away, but she thought about it all the next day. And the day after that. Each night she would lie on the rug at his feet, before the screen with all the colors and sounds. She was less and less worried about her children. It now seemed as if she and the tall man were taking care of them together. But it was clear to her now that the tall man was sad and lonely. And one night she felt her mothering instinct welling up in her, and found that she wanted to comfort him. And the next time he reached down his hand, she let him pet her.

It felt strange at first, but then not strange at all. It was familiar. It was like the old woman's touch. The tall man was gently stroking and caressing her fur and she felt an enormous sense of joy welling up in her. Then he picked up a piece of clothes line and began dangling it before her, and suddenly Mabel found herself playing. She chased the clothes line madly back and forth, running about in circles. She hadn't played in so long. She'd been so busy worrying about her kittens and trying to keep them alive. She had had them when she was still a kitten herself, and never realized how much she missed this. Her kittens were all watching her in amazement. They had never seen her act like this.

Then, when she grew tired, she curled up at his feet again, and began to purr. She couldn't remember the last time she'd purred like this. But now it was all coming out, so loud and strong. There on the rug, at the tall man's feet, with all her children safe and happy around her, Mabel purred and purred and purred.

What is this strange feeling? she thought. How can I possibly be so happy? And then she understood. It's home. This is my home. I'm home.

(The light fades on him and goes out.)

Miss Havisham's Wedding Cake

CHARACTER & SETTING

There is one character, **MISS HAVISHAM**, an old woman in an old, moth eaten wedding dress, who speaks to us from a circle of light on an otherwise dark stage.

*(**MISS HAVISHAM**, an old woman in a moth eaten
wedding dress, speaks to us from a circle of light on
an otherwise dark stage.)*

MISS HAVISHAM.

So Miss Havisham is jilted on her wedding day, and
spends the rest of her life in a moth eaten wedding
dress, plotting her revenge against men, and she saves
her wedding cake. She's got this huge old wedding cake,
covered in cobwebs, rats have eaten it, ants, spiders crawl
in and out, roaches, it's sitting there on this big table,
the whole dining room is left the way it was, dust an inch
thick, dust webs, dust bunnies, filth, rotting food, the
silverware laid out, it's like she's frozen this moment in
time, her life is like a clock that stopped ticking on that
day, the moment she realized he wasn't coming, the
moment she could no longer delude herself that she
was loved, that love was somehow possible, that a world
in which one could love and be loved and trust another
person was a possible world. That whole reality, that
whole imagined reality in which love is possible, it died,
the moment she realized he wasn't coming, and the
clock stopped, and something died in her, died in her
eyes, and from that moment on, reality was something
else, something much darker, in which the only thing
one could hope for was a kind of dark revenge. The
only joy one could take would be in causing someone
else to feel the pain that she'd felt, the horrible sense
of violation, that moment when suddenly the person
you've trusted throws shit in your face, when all of what
you've cherished turns out to have been a delusion, to
make somebody else feel that. That horrible sense of
humiliation and betrayal. This is what interests me.

And she goes to enormous lengths, incredibly
elaborate lengths to achieve this objective. She adopts

the prettiest little girl she can find and then teaches her to break hearts, and then she finds a boy, a poor boy, someone she can have completely in her power, so the little girl can practice on him, and observing with the fascination of a praying mantis about to eat her lover's head, like this big, cobweb covered insect, Miss Havisham watches as the boy falls hopelessly in love with Estella, the little girl she's molded into this seductive monstress, and then she watches him suffer, and suffer, and suffer, and she's fascinated.

And it isn't that she's not fond of this boy, because I think a part of her is fond of him. And it isn't that she doesn't feel sorry for him, because I think a part of her must feel sorry for him, but she can't help herself. She's got to watch. It's so fascinating. It's like a distorted backwards image of what happened to her.

And does it give her pleasure to watch him suffer? I think yes. I think it's clear that it does give her pleasure. If we have been made to suffer, it does give us pleasure to somehow gather up enough power to make another creature suffer. And in the suffering of the other creature we see our own suffering and humiliation mirrored, and we are able to step out of that role of the victim, which we have felt trapped in, since the moment of our discovery that reality is not what we'd hoped it was, that reality is in fact made entirely of betrayal, and we distance ourself from any feeling of sympathy, of identification we might instinctively have with the victim, and we take on the role, put on the mask, as it were, of the person who has the real power, the person who is loved, the person who has the power to accept or reject, and when the other person, the victim, the image of our former pathetic self, comes, heart in hand, beating in one's hands, bleeding through one's fingers, to give to us, we harden our heart, as it says in the Bible, we harden our heart and identify with the tormentor, the betrayer, and in this way we take on the betrayer's power, the power of the one in the relationship who loves less. The more we love, the more we make ourselves a victim.

But the question is, although it does give Miss Havisham a certain amount of sadistic pleasure to watch the boy suffer, to watch her creation, the beautiful Estella, make the protagonist undergo all the most exquisite torments of hell, the fellow who is a stand in for the bastard who left her at the altar, is Miss Havisham really comforted by the suffering she has caused? She watches him suffer the torments of the damned with a kind of dark, reptilian sexual excitement, and yet when she goes back to lie in her moldy chamber that night, alone, as she is alone, and will be alone, every night of her life until she dies, there in her moth eaten wedding dress, does she lie in the darkness giddy with happiness?

Of course she doesn't. Because the satisfaction she feels in her revenge is hollow. It is momentarily intense, but it is always false. She suffers. She makes someone else suffer. But she doesn't feel better. She is trapped in that falling apart, cobweb covered haunted house which is the place our soul goes to wither and rot, where there is no love, no intimacy and no hope, and she cannot be comforted. There is no comfort in this foul rag and bone shop.

But here is what really interests me in all this. Her attempt is to stop time. She feels that if she preserves the wedding cake, keeps wearing the wedding dress, changes nothing in the dining room and very little in the rest of the house, and sets up a kind of eerie, reversed reenactment of her betrayal and humiliation, that she can somehow conquer time, make time the illusion we would like it to be, even reverse time, through the staging of her horrible little passion play by which she hopes to achieve her revenge. Miss Havisham is an artist, really. She's a playwright, like God. And she hopes, through the instrument of her perverse art, to achieve a kind of salvation, as it were.

To conquer, to triumph against all odds. To redeem the world through art.

And of course she fails. Because the sad truth no artist wants to face is that we are not redeemed by art. It does not save us. We still suffer our pathetic and humiliating decay and ultimate dissolution. We are still eaten by maggots, like the worms in her wedding cake. Art does not save us. All art is an attempt at revenge, against those who have abandoned us, betrayed us, stopped loving us, ridiculed us, tormented us. And all art fails because art cannot love us. Art cannot love us. It cannot make us feel loved. Even when our art is appreciated by those around us, even if they should call us a genius, give us money, give us awards, it cannot make us happy. It cannot comfort us. It cannot hold us. It is not intimacy. It is all just a foul, stinking, moldy wedding cake, crawling with vermin.

Art is a lie, like love is a lie. That is what Miss Havisham knows, sitting in the dark, at four o'clock in the morning, staring at that pathetic and disgusting mass of putrefaction which was once the symbol of her innocence, and her hope for love. Her wedding cake is like a mirror. She looks at it and sees the reflection of her own inevitable putrefaction.

And time is not conquered. She has not stopped time. Because she is old. Her hands are old. Her eyes are old. She sees her reflection in the fly spotted mirror and there is a hideous old hag looking back at her, a person who is to her utterly unrecognizable. She has not stopped time. She has not achieved happiness through revenge. Her art has failed her. She sees it now as a pathetic waste of her time, of her life.

And yet, she thinks, is it possible for a human being not to waste her time? Because time is almost by definition waste. Time is a waste land. We can't hold onto it. It slips through our fingers, like all our illusions.

And yet, Dickens, the brilliant, slobbering, sentimental, grotesquely hypocritical genius who is the God of the novel she is trapped in, has supplied two endings to the story. In one ending, the boy goes back to Estella, and she is just as cruel and shallow as ever. She does not love him. She cannot love him. She'd rather go down to the docks in the fog and give herself to Long John Silver than let the boy so much as touch her hair. He is miserable, and she is miserable, and there is no love and no hope.

Or, there is the other ending. The ending in which the boy goes back to Estella and finds that she is lonely and unhappy in the role Miss Havisham has cast her in. That if he is very patient and very good to her, that she is, perhaps, after all, actually capable of loving him. That if one is kind and patient and good and forgiving and loves with all one's heart and all one's soul, loves without hope, simply loves with every fibre of one's being, then, in the end, it is possible, at least remotely possible, that one's love, finally, will be returned. That the beloved will at some point finally agree to join him in the mutual delusion of love, to share the neurotic dementia of imagined mutual love with the boy. That, in short, a happy ending is possible.

Now, life teaches us, as it has taught Miss Havisham, that this is ridiculous. That there are no happy endings. That most love ends in betrayal and disillusion, and all love ends in death. Youth turns to crabbed age. Hope turns to despair. Beauty to ugliness. Tenderness to hopeless grief and humiliation. All sane people know this.

And yet she cannot throw out the wedding cake. Why can't she throw out the wedding cake? Because she has continued to love. Why has she continued to love? Nobody knows. A saner person moves on to the next delusion. But Miss Havisham does not move on. She gets older, and uglier, and sadder, but she does not move on. And perhaps she envies those shallow souls who are capable of moving on, of moving from one delusional attachment to another until one finally reaches the point at which nobody is left who is stupid enough or ugly enough to imagine that they love you.

She is alone and she grieves because she still loves. She is the living image of what it is to love. Love endures no matter what. Love is dementia. And that is what she has come to. Now, in her old age, alone in the big, empty house, with just the rats and the vermin in her wedding cake, she has settled, finally, permanently, into the dementia she has in fact never ceased to embrace.

An owl hoots out her window. Rats scuttle in the walls. Miss Havisham sits down at the table, cuts herself a piece of cake, and begins to eat.

(The light fades on her and goes out.)

LAMENTATIONS
OF THE
BOGEYMAN

CHARACTER & SETTING

There is one character, the **BOGEYMAN**. Perhaps he is tall, wearing a long, black coat, with a hood. Or perhaps he looks quite different. Perhaps he speaks from the shadows. Maybe we don't even see him. He manifests himself differently in different cultures, but he is everywhere.

(The **BOGEYMAN** *speaks to us from the shadows.)*

BOGEYMAN.

Unspeakable loneliness,
lurking under the bed,
hiding in the broom closet,
waiting to jump out
from behind the dresser,
always in the shadows,
creature of darkness,
feared and despised,
monstrous, cannibal,
unholy thing.

I can almost remember
being somebody else.

In the old days
they were little monkey things
that lived in the trees
and I walked below,
in the jungle,
in the night,
in the dark,
waiting
for somebody
to fall.
To fall asleep.
To fall.

Now I'm mostly
trapped in houses.
It's like living
in a coffin.

A house like
a rabbit warren.
During the day,
alone in the house,
in a sea of ticking clocks,
smelling of mold
and moth balls,
I lurk in the attic,
gazing into dark,
fly speckled mirrors,
trying to remember
the words to "Stardust."

They used to play
the Nat King Cole version
all the time, but now
nobody remembers.

I like the Willy Nelson version too,
and the Louis Armstrong,
but it's a mistake to sing it too fast,
or play around with it too much,
and people who
skip the verse
should be killed.
The verse is what makes
the refrain so powerful.
It's the set up that makes
the punch line work,
just like it's being afraid
that makes them
most excited.
Fear is the foreplay
of all significant
experience.
It's the quality

of the foreplay
that makes the climax
so intense.

But what is the climax?
Is there a climax?
Do you hold back forever,
like Tantric sex?
Or does somebody devour
somebody's head?

How did he write this song?
How could something that odd
and that perfect
drip out the smoke-stained
yellow shaking fingers
of one whorehouse
piano player?
Under a red light bulb.
In a room full of
clotted ash trays
and empty
brown beer bottles.
Cigarette hanging out
of his mouth.
Liquor on his breath.
Hasn't shaved.
Suddenly, pouring out of him,
out his fingers, this
amazing thing.
Where does it come from?

It's a song about memory,
about how music
when soft voices die,
vibrates in the memory.

That's Shelley.

His pretty little wife
wrote *Frankenstein.*
I've seen the movie
from behind the sofa
in the dark
as the babysitter
copulates with
her rotten boyfriend
in the eerie glow
of the television set.

I'm so lonely.
Even Frankenstein
had a bride.
She hates me, says Frank.
Such sadness in his eyes.
Boris, trapped
in his makeup
and big shoes
with bolts in his neck
forever.

I am deeply in love
with Elsa Lanchester,
despite the
lightning bolt
hair style.
She is the pretty little author
at the beginning, and then
the sexy electric monstress
at the end
and I long to
see her naked.

But she's gone.
She's a shadow, like me.
I can't touch her.

Everybody's made of stardust.
Everybody's a temporary
coagulation of
intergalactic
dust bunnies.

I watch the copulations
of the meat puppets
with such longing,
so much jealousy
and anger.

So lonely.
I want to touch
somebody.

It isn't fair.
Her green eyes.

Why is it like this?
Why always this same
nightmare?

What crime have I committed?
Sometimes I look in the mirror
and don't see anything.
Smoke. Blurs.
I'm a blur in a fly speckled
mirror in the attic.

But just behind me.
Something lurking
behind me.
Frightens me.
What is it?
What is this feeling?
Fear.
I'm afraid.
What is it?

What's watching?
What's behind me?
Something I can't
quite remember.
Perhaps it is only
my reflection
in another mirror.

The most terrifying thing
is children.
Children terrify me most.
There is nothing
more terrifying
than children.
Because one knows
they will never
be loved enough.

The only reason love exists
is to torment us
when it's taken away from us.
And that's what we're
really most terrified of.
That there is no love.
That there will never
be any love.

Nobody will ever
touch us, or,
having been touched,
nobody will ever
touch us again.

Slack jawed cretins.
Stupid meat puppets.
Don't they know
what they've got?
Why do they get

the comfort
of warm flesh on flesh
while I am trapped here
smelling of moth balls?

I'll fix them.
I'll fix the bastards.
I'll scare the living
crap out of them.

I want to touch
so desperately.
I reach out into the darkness
I reach out my clawlike hand,
fingers trembling,
horrible, horrible,
to touch her—

    (Pause. Quietly. Sadly.)

Booo.

    (Darkness.)

Yeti

CHARACTER

There is one character, **JULIET**, a young woman of 30.

SETTING

The setting is a tent on a mountain in the Himalayas. It is night, during a snowstorm. All we can see is the lamp she sits by, her face illuminated by the light. All around her is darkness.

(Sound of wind blowing. Lights up on a small lamp in a tent surrounded by darkness. Night on a mountain. **JULIET** *in the tent, her face illuminated by the light.)*

JULIET.

Out there.

It's out there.

I can feel it.

It's moving around outside the tent.

The wind blows harder.

It's been following us.

Stalking us.

One by one,

the others disappear.

We shouldn't have come here.

This place is not ours.

We've taken everything else.

The rest of the earth.

This is the only place

they have left.

It's a terrible thing

to be where you're not wanted.

To be the intruder.

I've felt that before.

In a house where

I wasn't welcome.

With somebody

who wasn't interested.

Which is why I do

things like this.

Which is why I would come

to a place like this.
Some terrible loneliness
that compels one
to seek out lonely places.
To see it in a person's eyes.
He doesn't want you there.
It's horrible.
At night I dream of falling.
Into a bottomless abyss.
I never should have come here.
But I wanted to be with him.

I'm sure he didn't want me here.
But he doesn't like to make scenes.
I left him no choice.
Either make a scene
or let me come with him.
And I'm good at this.
I'm a good climber.
Nobody ever had to
wait on me.
My presence was never
a danger to anybody.
And I'm sure at night
he was happy
to have me curled up
in the tent with him.
But I might as well
have been anybody.
I was just a warm body.
His mind was already
someplace else.
It wasn't long after
we set out
that I knew something

was out there.
Following us.
I said nothing.
But I knew.
I didn't want him to think
because I'm a woman
I'd be imagining things.
But then the weather
got worse.
And we had trouble
counting each other.
And one by one
the others disappeared
in the snow.
And I fell asleep
in the tent
and when I woke up
he was gone, too.
And now it's just me
and the thing that's
been following us.
God knows how long
they've lived up here.
Long ago
we were the same animals.
But then we got separated.
That must be what happened.
And our group took over the world.
And their group retreated
to lonely places.
We were the aggressive ones.
The restless ones.
We were never satisfied.
They bred less.

Just wanted to be
left alone, in a quiet place.
So there were more and more of us,
and less and less of them,
until there were only a few
of them left,
up here in the mountains.

I know it's out there.
Just outside the tent.
What is it waiting for?
Is it lonely, like me?
What does it want from me?
Just to be left alone?
I've always felt alone.
Men have desired me
but nobody has loved me.
Some have imagined they did.
But they didn't know me.
They loved what they saw.
They didn't look inside.
They made up the woman
they thought they loved.

But I've never been drawn
to men who loved me.
I've always been drawn
to the other ones.
The ones in whose eyes
there was a certain coldness.
Desperately craving warmth
I have been hopelessly drawn
again and again
to the cold.
I don't know what's wrong
with me. I don't know

if it's my fault.
I suppose it must be.

Do these creatures love?
I think they must love.
And why has the creature
picked off each of the others,
and saved me for last?

I feel as if this place
were the only place in the world.
As if all of my life
leading up to this point
were a kind of dream.

Whatever is here, is there.
Whatever is there, is here.
Whoever sees here and there
as different places
meets death after death.

Have I come here to die?
Or have I come here because
somehow, I knew
something was waiting
for me here?

This creature,
this pathetic,
bearlike thing,
how long have they
been up here?
How lonely it must
have been for them.
We have our cities and
the magic of our
long distance
communications.

The labyrinth of our
despair.
But here in the cold
they have been waiting.
So long. What
are they waiting for?

For us to destroy ourselves?
So they can pick off
the survivors,
one by one.

But perhaps this one,
the one who is following me,
perhaps this creature
wants me for
some other purpose.
Perhaps the creature's loneliness
is much like mine.

I might love such a creature,
as long as I could look into its eyes
and see the cold there.
But if I saw love
in the creature's eyes,
I could not love it.
And it would see
that I could not love it.

They're right to shun us.
They're right to pick us off
one by one
when we get too close.
As I have picked off
everyone
who comes too close to me.

I dreamed I looked into
the darkness.

Into the red pit of Hell.

I am the victim of passion.
Pride has led me
a strange dance.

But sometimes I dream
of somebody I was
in another life.
In that narrow passage
between sleep and waking,
between life and death,
we remember, just for a moment
having passed ourselves
in the long hallway,
going out, coming back.

And sometimes falling
I get confused,
I can't remember.
I ask myself,
what am I?
What is this place?
What am I doing here?

And in my dream
the avalanche covers me,
there is something on top of me,
something lies on top of me,
protecting me,
some lost creature,
something that loves me.

It's out there in the snow.
It's waiting.
It's waiting for me.
Perhaps I should
invite the creature in.

(The lamp flickers and goes out. Darkness, and the sound of the wind.)

THE DESCENT
OF MAN

CHARACTER

There is one character, **MALONEY**, a man of forty.

SETTING

The setting is an American classroom in the first decade of the twenty-first century.

(**MALONEY**, *a man in his forties, in his classroom.*)

MALONEY.

Welcome to science class. I'm Mr Maloney. I will be impersonating your teacher today. As you've probably heard by now, things are going to be a little different this year. The school board, in its intergalactic wisdom, has decreed that in addition to the usual scientific curriculum, this year I am ordered, on pain of death, to teach parallel lessons on Creationism, which some persons prefer to call Intelligent Design, but since intelligence has in fact very little to do with it, I'm not going to call it that. But as a dedicated teacher who would not like to end up selling defective automobiles for Crazy Stan the Used Car Man, I am obliged to do whatever the school board decrees, however hopelessly stupid it may be.

So. What is Creationism? Creationism is the theory—I am instructed to refer to it as a theory, not a belief—Creationism is the theory that the universe, everything we see before us, was created by a Supreme Being, an idea with which you're no doubt already familiar from your lifelong involuntary participation in the primitive rituals which are routinely celebrated at your various places of worship. Blood drinking, flesh devouring, chicken sacrificing, that sort of thing.

Science, on the other hand, is perhaps something with which you are a bit less familiar. I'm not referring to your familiarity with all manner of complex and I might even say rather magical technology, much of which, even as a science teacher, I don't pretend to understand beyond a certain rudimentary level. But knowing how to manipulate this technology is not the same as having a good understanding of the scientific principles upon which it is based. Unless of course your theory is that God invented the portable electronic device you are all surreptitiously staring at or longing to stare at while pretending to listen to me.

When I was your age, in the era of the Bic pen, I used to surreptitiously stare at the perfectly formed legs of the girl sitting in front of me, who up until three weeks ago was my wife. She has recently upgraded to a newer and more powerful model. A stock broker with perfect teeth, excellent muscle tone, and a brain the size of a walnut.

She accused me of drinking too much, which is true, although in my defense if you were married to her, you'd drink too much, too. She said I was compulsively self-destructive. Which is not true. I don't want to die. I just want to go to sleep and wake up in a better place. Which is what people who believe in Creationism want. When they die, they want to wake up in a better place. They want to believe there is such a place. In science, however, what we want has absolutely nothing to do with anything. Science is about what's there whether we want it to be or not.

I got her pregnant in a Chevy, and that's why she married me. Not because it was a Chevy, but because she was pregnant. I really loved that Chevy. It was the best night of my life. It's been all down hill from there. After we got married, and after her miscarriage, her story became that I got her drunk and took advantage of her. This is another example of belief over evidence. Much like Creationism. If I was really self destructive, when the school board informed me I'd be required to teach Creationism in my science class, I'd have told them to shove their medieval curriculum up their fat, red ignorant asses. But I did not. Because I am not compulsively self destructive. I just have no self respect whatsoever.

And so I stand here before you, to share with you everything I know about that grotesque stew of superstition, ignorance and fairy tales which is the theory of Creationism. Not because I think it's anything but horse pucky. But because the school board made it clear they will fire me if I don't. And if they fire me, I won't be able to pay my alimony. So I'm doing this as a favor to my ex-wife and her lover, the amazing talking walnut.

As one particularly fat and stupid school board member put it, We don't want to pay our property tax to support a school where you stand up there and tell our children they're descended from monkeys. Which is absolutely not true. I have never told anybody they were descended from monkeys. I'm telling you you're related to monkeys. Although in fact you're much more closely related to the great apes. It's the difference between having parents who are monkeys and having distant cousins who are monkeys.

Nor have I ever asserted that the members of the school board are descended from monkeys. That would be an insult to monkeys. The school board is dumber than monkeys. The school board is dumber than egg plant. And they want me to help make their children dumber than egg plant, so they can all sit around and fart together in imaginary Heaven, playing the banjo with the kid from *Deliverance* and good old imaginary plastic Jesus. They want me to teach you that men and dinosaurs existed at the same time, along with Raquel Welch in her fur bikini and the Flintstone family.

And to be fair to them, I actually don't think their dinosaur theory is as stupid as it sounds. I don't think there's absolute evidence that every single dinosaur on the face of the earth was wiped out before human beings showed up. I mean, birds are dinosaurs, and dragon legends have got to have come from somewhere. A handful of thunder lizards here and there in remote areas surviving into the dark ages does not seem to me to be entirely out of the question. I try to keep an open mind. Isn't that what scientists are supposed to do? It's part of the scientific method.

Of course, scientists can be as patronizing, arrogant, selfish and narrow minded as the next fellow, and have had a tendency, over the centuries, to use the current scientific orthodoxy to suppress new theories and protect their territory. But this is just because human beings, on the whole, are dumb assholes. Even the smart ones. The scientific method is still the only way of investigating the world, with the possible exception of artistic creation, which is not essentially a fantastic mixture of superstition and bigotry. But America is the capital of superstition and bigotry. Hence this course.

The scientific method is a systematic approach to investigating how the apparent world around us works. One collects observations of events which seem to follow certain other events, and eventually one develops a hypothesis, that is, a possible explanation, of what appears to be happening, based not upon what one would like to be the case or has been told is the case but strictly upon one's observations of what would appear to be a cause and effect relationship.

Let's say I have observed that persons who step in front of charging rhinos tend to get their epiglottis ripped out. I see person after person stepping in front of charging rhino after charging rhino, and in each case, the person gets his epiglottis ripped out. On the basis of these long term repeated observations, I form the hypothesis that if you step in front of a charging rhinoceros, you will get your epiglottis ripped out, and as this hypothesis seems to be confirmed over and over again, I may feel justified in putting forth a theory, let's call it The Charging Rhinoceros/Epiglottis theory, which we may find useful until such time as somebody begins to observe that persons who stand in front of charging rhinoceri sometimes do not get their epiglottis ripped out, in which case we will have to try out a new hypothesis and perhaps revise or even discard our theory. That's how science works. Religion is not like this. Religion tells you what to believe so you don't have to think about it any more, and you don't have to pay attention to anything. And the last thing the school board wants you to do is think. God forbid that anybody around here might actually be forced to use their brain. That could result in the end of America as we know it.

My ex-wife, Felicity, says I say things like this because I secretly want to be fired. Felicity has always been a lot more fun when she's naked. And sometimes I wonder if she isn't right. If I can just piss these cretins off enough to go to the trouble of firing me, then I can blame them for the fact that I'm such a ridiculous fuck up. But I would just like to make it clear that I am not a ridiculous fuck up. I am a very serious fuck up. Look, you don't really believe all this sanctimonious bullshit, do you? Do you really think a benevolent deity created the world? What scares me is that probably you do.

Did you know that a higher percentage of Americans believe in Creationism than in Bulgaria? I don't mean that Americans don't believe in Bulgaria. I mean a higher percentage of Bulgarians believe in Evolution than Americans. I don't mean that Bulgarians don't believe in Americans. Maybe I should move to Bulgaria. I'm sure my ex-wife would be thrilled.

She says I'm acting like a child. But it's the religious people who act like children. That's what religion is: a desperate retreat into childhood. A fantasy world where we substitute what we'd like to be the case for what actually appears to be the case. Science is a hard sell to the stupid because it doesn't care what we want. It's a rational way of investigating a universe that would appear not to give a shit what happens to us. But we don't want that to be the case. We want to live forever with Daddy in a big house in the sky. God is a name you give to your fear and your ignorance. We don't understand what's going on here so we'll call it God and pretend it's our father and loves us and cares about us. That's childish. And yet I'm being paid to teach my students a bunch of fairy tales believed by cretins who are too scared to actually use their brains for anything but filling up the vacuum between their ears.

Felicity says that's arrogant. She says I'm never going to convince anybody of anything when I treat people with that sort of contempt. But people who want to pay me to shovel bullshit down their children's throats deserve my contempt. Well, maybe not my contempt. They deserve somebody's contempt. She says we don't get to decide what we teach our students. That our job is to teach what we're told to teach. Nobody's forcing me to be a teacher here, she says. We can't have every teacher deciding on their own what they're going to teach.

Why not? Why the hell not? Because that would be chaos, she says. But you should learn about chaos. There world is almost entirely made up of chaos. I'd love to teach chaos theory, except those brain dead zombies on the school board would probably want me to stick the Four Horsemen of the Apocalypse in there somewhere.

Not that I think there's anything wrong with them wanting you to get a bit of a moral foundation somewhere or other. God knows, you're going to need it. But science can't tell you how to behave. It can tell you what'll happen if you drop a bowling ball and a golf ball out the window at the same time, but it can't tell you what the right thing to do is. And it shouldn't try, because science is not about morality. Morality is a subjective human issue. Science is neither moral nor immoral. It's just a rational means of investigation in a largely irrational society.

Did you ever play Circle of Fools at a party? Everybody sits in a circle and one person whispers a story to the person beside them, who then whispers it to the person beside them, and you go all around the circle, and by the time it gets to the last person, it has little or no relationship to the story you started with. Well, evolution is like that, over incredibly vast amounts of time. You start with one thing and through a process of gradual alteration you end up with something else. What you end up with depends on what random mutations allow certain living things a better chance of surviving. The mutations are random, but what survives is not. Mutations are just mistakes in copying the genetic code, like typographical errors, but some mistakes actually produce creatures who are better able to survive, so they're the ones that reproduce. Unlike me. I do not reproduce. I just pay alimony and drink.

The theory of evolution relies on the fact that vast, nearly unimaginable epochs of time lie behind us, that life has altered itself and developed into us over these incredibly vast eons, generation by generation, tiny variations reproducing themselves. So the congressman who goes on television and announces with a smirk on his face that he's never seen a monkey turn into a person and feels that somehow he's disproved the theory of evolution is like an infant who believes you vanish when you play peek a boo. He's based his theory on a complete and possibly willful misunderstanding of the situation. Ignorance is forgivable. If a man is merely ignorant, he can learn. But if he's deliberately spouting bullshit so he can get re-elected by his ignorant constituents, he's the lowest form of sewage.

Ironically, the same people who reject evolution believe in the economic survival of the fittest. It's called the Protestant ethic, although you don't have to be a Protestant to be stupid. This idea, brought over by the Puritans, is that if you've got money, you deserve it, because God's rewarding you for being one of the elect. And if you don't have money, it's evidence that you don't deserve it, because God's punishing you. In other words, what matters in society, according to this essentially Fascist theory, is that those who already have money or those who are prepared to acquire money and power by any means necessary, are those that deserve to survive. They are God's chosen.

These people identify themselves as Christians, although they seem to reject just about everything Jesus said about the likelihood of being able to stuff a camel through the eye of a needle. They identify a free market as a market that's rigged to service the rich, powerful and ruthless at the expense of the poor, the sick, and the powerless. If the poor can't feed themselves, it's all part of God's plan. They'll get their reward, if they deserve it, in Heaven. In other words, the whole basis of the free market theory is that God is a gigantic ass hole, like J. P. Morgan.

But I have a confession to make. Since my wife left, I've been hearing these voices. It spooked me out so much I dropped my cell phone in the toilet. But it wasn't the cell phone. It was whispering in my head. I don't know if it's God or the Devil or what it is, but the voices tell me that reason itself is as pathetic, arrogant, and ultimately as futile as blind faith. Maybe you people are right. Maybe if I'm going to give in and teach Creationism then I should go all the way, buy an abacus and rely on shouting for long distance communication.

But just tell me this: Do you really want to believe in a God who's responsible for centuries and centuries and centuries of unspeakable carnage, the relentless slaughter of the innocent, of hunger, grief, unspeakable physical and emotional suffering, severed limbs, eyes gouged out, dead children, grieving mothers, devouring, devouring, devouring. Do you want to call that God? Is that your idea of an all powerful, benevolent God? The filthy son of a bitch who murdered my child?

Easier to believe it's all random selection. Easier to believe its an impersonal and meaningless process.

Not the pathetic delusion of an allegedly benevolent deity who loves us. A deity who loves us? A homicidal maniac. A fucking homicidal maniac.

(Pause.)

But I am required by the school board to tell you the story of the world according to the disciples of this homicidal maniac. So let us begin at the beginning.

In the beginning, God created the heavens and the earth. And the earth was without form and void. Just like us.

(The light fades on him and goes out.)

Fragments

CHARACTER & SETTING

There is one character, **DELLA**, a woman in her forties, who speaks to us from a circle of light surrounded by darkness.

(**DELLA**, *a woman in her forties, speaking to us from a circle of light, surrounded by darkness.*)

DELLA.

Every night I cook his meals for him. I put the food on his plate and he eats it. Have a little more gravy, I say to him.

He used to talk a lot. He talks less now. I'll tell you a secret, he said to me. It's not the gas. It's the land. You buy up the land dirt cheap. People don't know what it's worth. They need the money. Nobody else wants it. The harder times are for people the better it is for a land grab. Poverty is good for business.

You dig wells everywhere. Some hit. Some don't. Then you sell the land to some other company for more than you paid for it. That's how you make your money. Reselling the land. Then you move on.

He's very good at what he does. Everybody likes him. He's got a kind of down to earth, folksy charm these people can relate to. They're used to doing business with a handshake. If a fellow looks you in the eye, and shakes your hand, you know he's one of your own.

Just give them the money and tell them what they want to hear. Tell them it will be environmentally friendly, minimally invasive is a good phrase, because it makes them feel reassured but doesn't actually mean anything. And with the royalties, they'll be set for life. That's what he leaves them thinking.

He used that same folksy, earnest charm to seduce me in the back seat of his Oldsmobile, when we were teenagers. I recognize it. He seduces these people the way he seduced me.

73

Then before they know what's happening, the driveway is full of trucks, they've bulldozed the wooded hillside behind their house, and put up a gas rig five hundred feet from their kitchen door.

Fortunately, poor people are stupid, he said to me, lying in bed one night... That's why they're poor. It's not my fault if people are stupid, he said. Everybody's got to make a living.

Now they've got water you can light on fire right out of the faucet, a house they can't sell for any amount of money, their kids are sick, they're sick, and their royalty check is seventy-five dollars. It would have been more, the company tells them, but we've taken out most of it for additional expenses. That can mean anything. Read your contract. You signed it. Make the fine print really boring and show them some money and smile at them, and people will sign anything.

It's survival of the fittest, he said. And it's good for the country. And that's what makes me proud to be an American.

Here's what actually happens. The well casings fail, and hundreds of thousands of gallons of water full of carcinogenic chemicals gets into creeks and streams, and almost everything in the water dies. Catfish, salamanders, small mouth bass, mussels, minnows.

Pressure from a new hydraulically fractured gas well forces gas into older wells and methane percolates up into the basements of people's homes, and the houses explode.

In Pennsylvania, a four hundred thousand gallon impoundment of waste water produced by hydraulic fracturing explodes. The flames are a hundred feet high. A black plume of smoke is visible for miles. It looks like a vision of Dante's Hell.

It's not his fault these poor hicks are greedy and stupid and gullible as puppies. You smile at them and talk folksy like somebody from their church and they'll trust you. They'll believe any damn bullshit you tell them if they like your handshake and there's money in your hand. They're not thinking down the road. They're thinking right now. And they don't trust them pansy environmentalist commies. They trust the smiling ass hole with the money.

And as for the death of their grandchildren, they don't think about that. They don't want to know about the toxic noodle soup of carcinogenic shit that ends up in their water supply, and thanks to our paid off friends in Congress, we don't have to tell them.

This is the best damned racket ever invented, he says to me.

And as for the decimated forests, the roads covered with endless trucks, going back and forth all day and all night, and the cancer in the water, we will not be paying for this. Somebody else will pay. We'll be gone. It's a beautiful racket.

As long as it's somebody else's land. Somebody else's water. Somebody else's cancer. Somebody else's dead grandkids. You look up and we're gone. Somebody else will take care of that.

And I just looked the other way. It gave us a good life. A nice house. A series of nice houses. A comfortable life. Until my first grandchild. Until my first grandchild was.

Watching her die. Watching that little girl die. I looked at that child, and for the first time I saw other people's children. I walked out of the hospital in a kind of dream, and we drove home in silence through one of the toxic wastelands he'd helped create. And I wondered what was in our water. I wondered what was in the children. And I looked at him, driving home through Hell, and I knew that I'd sold my soul for a few pieces of silver. And my grandchild was dead. And other people's grandchildren were dead. And the land was dead.

All this time, I looked the other way. I looked the other way. I looked the other way.

He hasn't been the same since. Whether he connects the two or not, the death of his grandchild, and the deaths of other people's children, the death of the land, I don't know. He doesn't talk about it. He doesn't talk at all. He hasn't been feeling well lately.

Every night I cook him his dinner. And every night I slip a little something special in it for him. A little bit of something they inject into those wells. And I watch him slowly turn yellow. I watch his eyes get darker. I listen to him throwing up at night. The doctors are baffled. They don't know what's wrong with him.

Finish your dinner, I say to him. I'll make you feel better, honey. Have a little more gravy.

(The light fades on her and goes out.)

EVENINGS
NEAR KIEV

The doors were torn from their hinges, and a numberless horde of monstrous creatures flapped their way into God's church.
– Nickolai Gogol, "Viy"

CHARACTER & SETTING

There is one character, **BEN**, a man in his sixties. He speaks to us from his study, late at night. Mostly darkness around him.

(**BEN**, *a man in his sixties, speaks from his study,*
late at night, surrounded by darkness.)

BEN.

Tonight they're killing protesters in Kiev, setting them
on fire. And all night, Gogol has been whispering to
me in the darkness. To his right, a wooden table upon
which sits an old lantern and a thick stack of the
handwritten manuscript of a novel. To his left, an old
potbelly stove. Behind him, an old, cracked mirror. A
dirty window. He is a craggy faced man with oily black
hair, a droopy black mustache, a big hooked nose, a
large mouth and wild, tormented eyes.

One should begin at the end, he says, but in fact one
is always opening the book in the middle and closing
it before one understands the story. Where do these
things come from? How can one be certain? I get
letters from God, but I can't read his handwriting. God
knows everything, but he's trying to forget. It's only
frightening the first time you die.

He's been living on spoonfuls of sauerkraut brine and
watery oatmeal soup. A few drops of wine in a tin cup
full of water. Everyone he knows is begging him to eat.
But he can't eat. He is almost finished with the second
part of *Dead Souls*, his masterpiece, the crowning
achievement of his life. Leave me alone, he says. I'm
fine. He prays all night to something monstrous out
the window, looking in.

For when, on a long winter's evening, when the spindle
whirs, and darkness gathers, something's scratching at
the door, and suddenly there are monsters everywhere,
an incredible confusion of voices and visions invade his
head from another place, causing him to make things.

I have always heard these voices. It was the holy strangeness of my childhood. They thought I was insane.

The bell in the morning, in Kiev. Dogs barking. Gogol says you can tell the King of the Gnomes because his eyelashes reach all the way to the ground. Greasy with a dirty nose, long black mustaches and a thick neck. A black eye. A fat lip. Clothes torn and dirty. They smell of tobacco and brandy. Everything in his pockets, all manner of rubbish, feather whistles, knucklebones, half eaten slices of pie, sparrows. Or am I looking in the mirror? he says. A mirror is the most dangerous object. It is a window into other dimensions. If you look in the mirror, you can see the Devil peeking over your shoulder.

Outside, he can smell something burning.

When I was a teenager, long before I ever heard of Gogol, I'd hole up in my room in the evenings and write for hours, a blue fountain pen in red College notebooks. Poems. Stories. Journals. And then when I'd filled up the notebook, I'd take it out back to the trash barrel and burn it. I burned everything I wrote. I was reading *A Moveable Feast* and *Let Us Now Praise Famous Men* and *King Lear,* and I was old enough to see clearly how ridiculous what I was writing looked compared to that. The idea that anybody would ever set eyes on what I'd written was horrifying to me. I can still see the pages burning. I suppose it was a kind of suicide.

The attic in Gogol's head is like a cherrywood puppet theatre. There is always some grotesque comedy playing there. Some nights he dreams of the dance of Salome. Bring me the head of Gogol, she says. Does he remember fornicating with the Queen of Spades? The cards are shuffled. And out of the hum of voices in his head like bees, a witch girl.

Watermelon, bubble lips and poppycock for sale. Porridge to pour on your head. Forbidden fruit. Lard to rub on your sister. Would you like to buy a honey tart, young man? It's still warm. I baked it myself. You may confiscate my pastry any time you like. Or perhaps you'd prefer a sausage? Are you fond of entry? What's that sticking out of your pants? Is that a carp? You could cut a woman in half with that thing. I have a hot pot of dumplings for you, sir. Jabbering and babbling. She won't shut up.

The darkness thickens. It's getting colder in the fields. Through the deep ravine and into the boggy weeds. The road is very muddy here, among the tangled briars. Cornfields sown with teeth. Playing cards nailed to the plum trees. The trees are mumbling to each other. Crawling over uneven ground. Dark as the Devil's fist. The Devil fancies he is a handsome fellow, while Gogol is ugly as sin. A faint groaning sound: the howling of the wolf? Two red eyes in the woods.

The child is afraid, alone in the forest. Blood drips from the trees. Where is the road? Get drunk and lie down like a dog in the weeds. We've lost our way in the wilderness of mirrors. The moon is not expected.

The great critic, John Ruskin, idolized the painter, Turner, but when he found hundreds of erotic drawings by Turner in the basement of the British Museum, images of all manner of copulation, Ruskin, whose pretty young wife had left him for a painter, took all those priceless drawings out and burned them.

Intolerable emptiness. I'd kill for some bread and dripping. I am haunted by the witch girl. I can't remember her face. No good can come from the Devil. When drawing something long and crooked out of a basket—

Look up at the stars above the trees in the cold, black night. A light appears in the darkness. A cottage in the forest. The creaking open of the gate. A coughing old woman, a shriveled face like a baked apple. Who's there?

Let us come in for the night, Granny. My stomach is empty, and I'm afraid to stay out of doors.

But what sort of people are you? What's that smell?

Harmless people. Students. Bring out the lard and pluck the chickens.

The house is full. You'll eat all the food. Students are worse than rats. There's no room here for you. No food. No fire. Nothing is given here. We don't want beggars who snatch carp off a wagon.

We'll pay for everything.

Yes. You'll pay. The Devil has brought you here, and you will pay. If it's the Devil you need, then go to the Devil. He will dip you in sour cream and slurp up your dumplings like noodles. The dumplings will be jumping in his mouth. But you must not sleep together. We'll put you in with the sheep.

After the great translator and explorer Richard Burton died, his wife took thousands and thousands of pages of his unpublished manuscripts and journals and burned them in the back yard. It was a kind of revenge, I think.

There's a pig looking in the window. The old woman comes to me at night with open arms, an open robe and lust in her heart. Her eyes flash with some extraordinary light. I try to push her away, but I can't move my arms, can't move my legs, nothing comes out of my mouth but drool. The words die on my lips. Listen to my heart beating.

She folds my arms, bends my neck, jumps on my shoulders like a cat, hits my ass with a broom and makes me run like a Cossack's horse. I grab my knees to try and stop my legs. Witch. It's a witch.

Coal black forest beneath us. A long plain bordered by a dark wood. A backwards half moon shines pale in the sky. The earth is sleeping.

First the old woman rides on Gogol. Then Gogol rides on her and beats her with a stick. Her cries, at first, like rage, and then more gentle, pleading, and then the sounds of pleasure. Can this really be an old woman? There is a rumor about someone's daughter. Somebody always has a pretty daughter, and that is the end of all happiness.

Is there a naked girl in the water? Lying before me is a beautiful maiden with long, white arms. No matter how many times you throw her in the water, she comes floating back to you. She is crying. She has the eyes of an old woman, but she is young, and she is dying. Do whatever she says, or you will be destroyed.

I see my reflection in the water over the grass, water nymph swimming there. She turns her back. Her breasts. Little bubbles on them, like beads. She trembles all over and laughs in the water. Just don't start kissing me, she says. Tell me why the moon shines.

They keep going into her bedroom and hiding in sacks. The Devil is in one of these sacks. The question is, which one? You open the sack, anything could jump out onto your neck. The moon flies out the chimney. The Devil sits on my neck. What have I done? Did I steal anybody's cow? I would sell my soul for her.

Awake and asleep are reflections in broken glass. Music in the wind, and chimes. Exorcism. Lightning illuminates. The earth flashes beneath me. We are falling. The trembling of the leaves in the trees. The trees are mumbling to each other. Then darkness, and oblivion.

In Florence, Savonarola made a huge mountain of books and paintings in the square and burned them, the bonfire of the vanities, and Botticelli cheered him on, Botticelli cheered him on. When we have reached a certain level of despair, our most precious creations seem to mock us. They are devices for God to make us suffer. And so we destroy them.

Long past midnight, near dawn, the barking of a dog. Outside the gates, two windmills turn. Windfallen apples. I awake to the whispering voices of old women. During the night, somebody's daughter died. Candles around a black coffin. Glancing sidelong at it. The dead girl is the witch. After you've seen a corpse, touch the stove.

Then she is sitting up in the coffin, all blue, eyes burning like coals. Looking into the dead girl's face. You are an evil thing, she says.

Encouraged by the crowing of the cock, she is standing before me, fixing her dead green eyes upon me, clacking her teeth together, reciting incantations and growling.

A small child walks to the coffin, as if hypnotized. She reaches for the child so tenderly, then grabs it, foam comes to her lips, she rips off its head, and starts drinking its blood. The blood drips down her chin, into a bucket. She laps blood from the headless corpse like a wolf. The mind darkens. Blood in my eyes. The laughter of demons. Now she is moving towards me.

To have become possessed by this evil thing, this living corpse, this old woman who is young and dead, by her green eyes, by the obscenity of story. Such horrors. Wings beat against the windows. Unclean powers flit all around him. A pack of howling wolves. An entire wall obscured by a huge monster standing amid its tangled hair like a forest. The wind sweeps through the church. The coffin flies through the air. It sucks her in. The coffin slams shut. Bang.

So the church remains forever with monsters stuck to its doors and windows, overgrown with roots, weeds and wild blackthorn. No one can find a path to it.

James Joyce tried to burn the first draft of *A Portrait Of The Artist*, and only his wife Nora, reaching into the flames, managed to save most of it. She couldn't read, herself, but she knew he was burning his soul.

It is dark, dark in my house now, and I am alone. There are so many doors in this place, but which one leads out? They all go to a place I don't want to be.

The raven sits on the stump. The rains will wash your bones. You get up in the night to pee, and when you come back to bed, something's come out of the mirror, a visitor from the swamp, with horns on his head, drags himself across the floor and begins strangling you. Or the Devil is curled up at the end of the bed, like a bundle, under the sheets.

At the goat's wedding, they ate the mandolins. The doves are in mourning. They will say, he died because he was afraid. If he hadn't been afraid, nothing would have happened to him. I am shaggy and gnaw my hands. Slowly I become invisible. Soon I will be entirely gone. No face. No body. Nothing. Only a pile of ashes.

A brothel at Nevsky Prospect. Where is Gogol? she cries. Somebody fetch Gogol. They bring in the head of a lamb on a platter. It looks at Gogol, and he knows it's the Devil. The Devil is sobbing in his hovel, frightened jackdaws rise in flocks. The Devil whispers in his ear. Gogol knows what he must do, that creation itself is evil, that the part of him from which creation springs is evil, that the voice he hears in his head is the Devil's voice.

He has finished writing the Second Part of *Dead Souls*. His masterpiece. Give up what you love, whispers the Devil, so the world can't take it from you. He takes the manuscript to the stove, opens it, throws it into the fire.

The Devil roasting sinners on a spit like sausages. Inside the big oven, under the pots. Fat dumplings with sour cream. A bearded goat on the roof. The Devil unties the knots, one by one, until the box is empty. Gogol is staring into the fire.

I sit here in an empty house, alone, my life's work all around me, and all of it seems a mockery. Tonight they're killing protestors in Kiev, setting them on fire.

I close my eyes and see a girl dancing naked for me in front of the mirror.

The stars disappear from the sky one at a time. The Devil is quietly sneaking towards the moon. The Devil burns his fingertips on the moon. The Devil has hidden the moon in his pocket. Nobody understands that the Devil has stolen the moon. The Devil has eaten the moon.

(The light fades on him and goes out.)

The Girl And The Crows

For Anna Contessa

CHARACTER & SETTING

There is one character, **JASMINE**, a young woman, who speaks from a circle of light, surrounded by darkness.

(Sound of crows cawing in the distance. Lights up on JASMINE, a young woman.)

JASMINE.

Once upon a time there was a girl who was afraid of crows. She couldn't remember a time when she hadn't been. She had a vague memory of being very small, and sitting on the ground, and a large crow flying towards her face, cawing, but she wasn't sure if that was a real memory, or if it was something she dreamed. She often dreamed about crows, and they were always terrible dreams, from which she'd wake up crying. She was also afraid of the dark, and it seemed to her that the crows flew out of the darkness. They lived in the dark and waited for her.

The girl was living with some people who didn't love her, and she was very much alone. There was a cornfield near the house where she'd been sent to live, and whenever she saw crows in the cornfield, she'd throw rocks at them, and chase the crows away. After a while, it seemed to her that the crows recognized her, and would watch her carefully. Sometimes when she'd take a walk down the railroad tracks, where she wasn't supposed to go, she'd look behind her, and there, sitting on the branch of a sumac tree, would be a crow.

After a while the girl became convinced the crows were following her, spying on her. Everywhere she looked, she thought there were crows, hiding around the corner. In the evening, when she saw the crows gathering over the cornfield, cawing, she thought they were talking about her, plotting against her.

And more and more she was afraid to go to sleep, because when she slept, she would dream about crows flying out of the mirror at her. In her dream, she would be looking at herself in the mirror, trying to understand who she was, and where she had come from, and where she could possibly be going, when suddenly the mirror would seem to darken, and then crows would be flying out at her, straight for her eyes. And in her dream, there was a sound like some terrible wheezing monster coming at her, and a shrill shrieking noise, and the girl would wake up trembling and drenched in sweat, and sobbing.

She had few memories of her parents. She wasn't sure what had happened to them, and nobody seemed interested in telling her. The people she lived with pretended to like her, but they were not very nice to her, and she knew they were just keeping her for the money they received to do so. Sometimes she would close her eyes and try to remember her mother's face, but she couldn't. She had a photograph but it was blurry. And her eyesight wasn't good. The world seemed to be getting darker and darker to her.

One day at sunset the girl was walking down the railroad tracks, very unhappy, when she heard a train approaching from behind her.

(Sound of a distant train approaching, faint at first, gradually growing louder.)

She turned to look, and she could see the train in the distance. She couldn't tell how fast it was coming. The sun was setting, and it was difficult to see. The train seemed to be coming at her from right out of the setting sun. She knew she should get off the tracks, but a voice in her head said, What does it matter? I'm all alone. Nobody loves me. Nobody will ever love me. So the girl just stood in the middle of the tracks and watched the train coming closer and closer to her.

(Train sound, getting closer and louder now.)

She could feel the ground shaking under her feet. The train was making a lot of noise, and the whistle was blowing louder and louder.

(Sound of the train whistle blowing.)

It was just like her dream. She wondered if she was dreaming, but she didn't think so.

Then, just as the train was almost upon her, there was a flapping of wings, and something flying at her from the side.

(Loud flapping noise.)

It was a crow, and it flew right at her face and buried its claws in her hair.

(Slapping at the invisible crow.)

The girl slapped at the crow as it went by, but the crow flew back at her from the other direction, and again she could feel its claws in her hair, and the wings brush against her face as it went by.

(The flapping noise again. She slaps at the crow. The train is closer.)

The third time the crow came at her, it was clear to her it was going right for her eyes, and she turned her head, and staggered off the tracks, just as the train went by, with a great roaring sound, and the shrieking of the whistle.

(She staggers off the tracks and falls. Roaring sound of the train as it goes by, and the whistle. Then gradually the sound diminishes and disappears.)

The girl lay in the weeds by the side of the track, her arms bleeding from her fall, but otherwise unhurt. She looked up, and there, sitting on a rock, was the crow, looking at her.

Why did you do that? said the girl. Why did you keep flying in my face like that?

Why do you throw rocks at us? said the crow.

Because you're horrible, said the girl. And I don't like you.

Why am I horrible? said the crow.

Because in my dreams you fly out of the mirror at me, said the girl.

You don't like me because of something in your dreams? said the crow. Does that really make sense to you?

I don't understand, said the girl. I thought crows were supposed to be intelligent. If you wanted me to stop throwing rocks at you, why didn't you just leave me alone, and let the train hit me? That wasn't very smart of you.

Perhaps not, said the crow.

Then why did you do it? said the girl.

The crow looked at her a while before it spoke.

You're a child, said the crow, finally. I have children.

The girl looked at the crow. The crow looked at the girl.

It's a trick, she said. Crows will trick you. I know about crows. You can't trust them.

Time to go home, said the crow, and flew away.

That night the girl dreamed that she went to look in the mirror, and saw that in her reflection there was a crow on her shoulder.

The next day, when the girl came to the cornfield, she didn't throw rocks. She just sat down in the dirt and watched the crows. After a while, the crows seemed to get used to her, and didn't pay much attention.

When she'd been there for a while, the crow from the railroad tracks came and landed near her.

Did you run out of rocks? said the crow.

No, said the girl. It's impossible to run out of rocks. I just decided not to throw any today.

The crow sat with her for a while, and they watched some smaller crows flying about playing.

Are those your children? asked the girl.

Yes, said the crow.

They're rather handsome children, actually, said the girl. For crows, I mean.

Yes, said the crow.

They watched the crows playing in the corn.

I dreamed about you last night, said the girl.

Did you? said the crow.

I was looking in the mirror, and you were on my shoulder, said the girl.

Was I? said the crow.

Yes, said the girl. I don't know what it means. Do you?

No, said the crow.

I've always been afraid of crows, said the girl. I've never had a happy dream about crows before.

Interesting, said the crow.

They sat there a while longer, not saying anything.

Thank you, said the girl. For what you did. Thank you.

You've got something in your hair, said the crow. And it hopped up onto her shoulder and pulled a wisp of corn silk from her hair.

The girl was startled, at first. But then she decided she didn't mind the feeling of the crow there on her shoulder.

You're not afraid to be on my shoulder? said the girl.

No, said the crow. It feels all right. Does it feel all right to you?

Yes, said the girl. I guess so.

Would you like to meet my children? said the crow.

Yes, said the girl.

She stood up carefully, with the crow on her shoulder, and walked across the field to meet the crow's children. And from that day on, and for the rest of her life, the girl was not afraid of crows, ever again.

(The light fades on her and goes out.)

Palimpsest

Instead of constructing whole objects, and waiting for time and chance to turn them into fragments, suppose I simply construct them as fragments to begin with, masquerading as recovered pieces of formerly completed objects which in fact never existed as such? What if I then reconstruct the imaginary original, then fragment it again, on purpose, only in a different way, so that different pieces remain, with some overlapping of the previous set of fragments? Then suppose I construct a revised text, somewhat different, and then fragment that, so that pieces of it which survive are some of them incompatible with the earlier fragments? And suppose I continue this process, constructing new wholes out of different variations of these fragments? Constructing greater and ever more complex insoluble enigmas for some future Martian literary archeologist. What then? Is this not what God has done? And is this no more or less futile an activity than ostentatiously picking one's nose in a snot factory? Oh, to be shut up in God's attic, with all the multitude of things he has forgotten.

– N. J. Drago, The Occult Notebooks

CHARACTER & SETTING

There is one character, **BEN**, a man in his early sixties, who speaks to us from his study, in his house by the woods, late at night.

(BEN, a man in his early sixties, speaks from the study of his house by the woods, late at night.)

BEN.

Palimpsest. Layer of old parchment. Dark scribblings, half erased, partially obscured by later scribblings. Tattered billboards, rain-drenched faces peering through rips. In my head, the past, past loves, showing through in the rain, touching each other. What lingers from one love bleeds into the next.

Love is a collage made up of past lovers, a palimpsest, images of old loves showing through, creating unexpected juxtapositions, unexpected meaning.

You say to one person what you realize you have said to others. You're not even aware of it at first. Over time, you realize, every love is a mosaic made of fragments of old loves.

You are the constant. Your pain. Your projection of the anima upon yet another girl. But in fact, all this time you have been alone. You have been the most alone when with someone you love.

But there is no going back to one's previous state of delusion. Once the veil is lifted, it's torn. You can't put it back. You can't unsee what you've seen. Which is a reality which has no relationship to what you desire or what you love.

So it's three o'clock in the morning, on New Year's Eve, and I'm driving through a blizzard with my friend. It's very dark and very cold, and the snow is hitting the windshield sideways like machine gun bullets, and it's very difficult to see what's coming, and the road is getting more and more slippery, a layer of ice under a fresh coating of snow.

The long night drive through relentless whiteness is a revelation to the Mexican girl. She is twenty six, very beautiful, intelligent, tender, funny, and she is absolutely enchanted by the snow.

I've never seen this, she says. I mean, I've seen snow, in New York, but I've never driven in a snowstorm, at night, in the dark like this. It's so beautiful. She watches, hypnotized, as I try to keep the car on the road, her young life in my hands.

Analogy is the key, to thought and to creation. We discover through a process of association: one thing brings to mind something else, and that's how we come to believe we understand something, characterize it, name it.

By the often apparently chance juxtaposition of fragments we discover analogies and correspondences we would not have otherwise suspected. This is why we shuffle the cards.

William Burroughs used to write with three radios on, turned to three different stations. This is the associational method.

And also, as one gets older, systematic reading gives way to following obscure paths through the labyrinth from odd book to odd book, echoes of childhood discoveries and unexpected new ones, these apparently chance juxtapositions resulting in new strange pathways to follow, until one is found dead under the sassafras tree, gnawed on by the woodland creatures one has been feeding.

The sky is a weird purplish pink color I've never seen before, and the lights we pass create a kind of eerie fog of snow around us. The snow on the ground is pure white, pristine, unsullied. We move through the driving snowstorm. I clutch the wheel, peering into the darkness, trying to keep the car on the road. This is so beautiful, she says again. This is like a dream. As one gets older, more and more, everything is like a dream, except for dreams. The dreams themselves seem real.

So are you a believer? she asks. Do you believe in God? Or anything?

I'm not by nature a believer, I said. Not a religious person. But I am drawn to the mystics, and Taoism and Buddhism, and sometimes it feels to me like there's a lot more going on around us than we're aware of. But I don't know that I believe anything. I'm drawn to animism. The sense that everything around us is alive. But I really don't know. When I write, I believe what the characters believe, while I'm inside them. But not afterwards.

I believe in ghosts, she says. I think there are spirits all around us.

I think of McTaggart, who always saluted cats in the street, and believed he had proven that time is an illusion, and the ultimate reality is the energy of immortal loving souls.

We drive through the snow. I glance over at her face. She's looking out the window. She is beautiful like a girl in a Vermeer painting. The dark is all around us. We move through the darkness towards oblivion.

I'm driving her to the airport, so she can spend New Year's Eve with someone she loves. Then I'll drive home in the snow.

Palimpsest. For a moment I am in touch with what I have felt in other lives. Women I have loved. Some now dead. There are layers and layers. The snow falls. The spirits are all around us. We move through them in silence, like a dream.

(The light fades on him and goes out.)